Sacred Events in Islam

Introduction

Islam is a faith filled with beautiful moments, special days, and meaningful events that help Muslims grow closer to Allah. Throughout the year, there are sacred months, blessed nights, joyful celebrations, and important historical events that remind Muslims of worship, kindness, gratitude, and faith. These moments are treasured by families and communities all around the world.

In this book, readers will journey through some of the most important events in Islam. From learning about the Islamic calendar to discovering the beauty of Ramadan, the joy of Eid, the sacred journey of Hajj, and the wonder of the Night Journey, each chapter explains why these occasions are so meaningful.

This book is designed to help children and families understand not only when these events happen, but also what lessons they teach. Some chapters focus on patience and prayer, while others highlight generosity, sacrifice, forgiveness, and acts of kindness. Together, they show how Islam guides both special celebrations and everyday life.

Islamic Calendar

The Islamic calendar is a special way Muslims keep track of the months and important days of the year. Unlike the calendar many people use every day, which follows the sun, the Islamic calendar follows the moon. Each new month begins when the new crescent moon is seen in the sky. This makes the Islamic calendar very special because it connects time with the beauty of the night sky and the signs created by Allah.

The Islamic calendar has twelve months, just like the solar calendar, but the months are slightly shorter because they are based on the moon's cycle. This means the Islamic year is about 354 days long, which is a little shorter than the 365 day solar year. Because of this, important Islamic events such as Ramadan, Eid al Fitr, Eid al Adha, and Hajj move through different seasons over the years.

The calendar begins with an important event in Islamic history called the Hijrah, the migration of Prophet Muhammad, peace be upon him, from Mecca to Medina. This journey marked the beginning of a strong Muslim community and became the starting point of the Islamic calendar. For this reason, the Islamic calendar is also called the Hijri calendar.

Understanding the Islamic calendar helps us see why Muslims celebrate and observe special days at different times each year. It teaches us that time itself can remind people of faith, worship, gratitude, and important moments in Islamic history. As you read this book, the Islamic calendar will guide you through the blessed months, sacred nights, and joyful celebrations that Muslims around the world treasure.

1447 H

Why Muslims Observe Special Days

Muslims observe special days throughout the year because these moments help them remember Allah, strengthen their faith, and reflect on important events in Islamic history. Some days remind Muslims of the lives of the prophets, while others celebrate acts of worship, kindness, sacrifice, and gratitude. These special times bring families and communities together in prayer, learning, and joyful gatherings.

Many of these days are connected to the Islamic calendar, which follows the moon. Because the months change with each new moon, the dates of Islamic events move through the seasons over time. This means a special day like Ramadan may come in winter one year and in summer many years later. Even though the season changes, the meaning of the event remains the same.

These observances also teach important values. Ramadan teaches patience, self control, and compassion for those who have less. Eid teaches joy, generosity, and sharing with family, friends, and neighbors. Hajj teaches unity, humility, and devotion, as Muslims from around the world gather together in worship.

By observing these special days, Muslims keep their traditions alive and pass them on to the next generation. Children learn why these events matter, families create cherished memories, and communities grow stronger in faith. As this book continues, each chapter will explore one of these important days and show how it helps Muslims grow closer to Allah.

Foundations

of

Faith

The Foundations of Faith are the core beliefs and practices that guide a Muslim's life. These teachings help Muslims grow closer to Allah, live with kindness, and build strong habits of worship. They are called the foundation because they support everything else in Islam, much like the base of a strong and beautiful building.

In this section, readers will discover the Five Pillars of Islam, the declaration of faith, daily prayers, charity, fasting, and the sacred journey of Hajj. Each chapter shows how these important acts shape the heart, strengthen the community, and connect Muslims to the special events and sacred times throughout the year.

The Five Pillars of Islam

The Five Pillars of Islam are the most important acts of worship that guide a Muslim's life. They are called "pillars" because they support the faith, just as strong pillars hold up a building. These five pillars help Muslims remember Allah, live with kindness, and stay connected to their beliefs every day.

The first pillar is Shahada, the declaration of faith, which means believing that there is no god but Allah and that Prophet Muhammad is His messenger. The second pillar is Salat, the five daily prayers that help Muslims remember Allah throughout the day. The third pillar is Zakat, giving charity to help those in need and to keep the heart generous.

The fourth pillar is Sawm, which means fasting during the month of Ramadan. Muslims fast from dawn until sunset, learning patience, gratitude, and self control. The fifth pillar is Hajj, the pilgrimage to Mecca, which every Muslim who is able should perform at least once in their lifetime.

These five pillars are the foundation of many of the important events in Islam. Ramadan is connected to fasting, Hajj is one of the pillars itself, and Eid celebrations often come after great acts of worship. By understanding the Five Pillars, readers can better appreciate why the special days in Islam are so meaningful.

Five Pillars of Islam

Shahada
(The Declaration of Faith)

The Shahada is the first and most important pillar of Islam. It is the simple but powerful declaration of faith that says, "There is no god but Allah, and Muhammad is the Messenger of Allah." These words are the heart of a Muslim's belief and remind Muslims to worship Allah alone.

When a person says the Shahada with sincerity and truly believes in it, they enter the faith of Islam. These words are often among the first things Muslim children learn because they form the foundation of everything else in the religion. The Shahada teaches trust in Allah, love for the prophets, and belief in the message of the Quran.

The Shahada is also connected to many important Islamic events and acts of worship. During Ramadan, Muslims fast because Allah has commanded it. During Hajj, pilgrims repeat words of faith and devotion. During the two Eids, Muslims gather in prayer and remember Allah together. In this way, the Shahada is present in every special time of the Islamic year.

More than just words, the Shahada guides the way Muslims live each day. It inspires honesty, kindness, gratitude, and devotion to Allah. By understanding the Shahada, readers can better see how all the important events in Islam are tied together by faith.

محمد
الله

Salat
(The Daily Prayers)

Salat is the second pillar of Islam and one of the most important acts of worship in a Muslim's daily life. Muslims pray five times each day, remembering Allah from morning until night. These prayers help keep the heart focused on faith, gratitude, and obedience.

The five daily prayers are spread throughout the day. Fajr is prayed before sunrise, Dhuhr at midday, Asr in the afternoon, Maghrib just after sunset, and Isha at night. Each prayer is a special moment to pause, thank Allah, and ask for guidance and forgiveness.

Salat is closely connected to many important events in Islam. During Ramadan, Muslims often pray even more, especially the special night prayers called Taraweeh. On Fridays, Muslims gather for the important Jumuah prayer. During Eid, large groups come together for joyful prayers, and during Hajj, pilgrims pray in the sacred places of Mecca.

These daily prayers teach discipline, peace, and closeness to Allah. No matter where Muslims are in the world, prayer brings them together in worship. By understanding Salat, readers can better appreciate the rhythm of faith that continues through all the sacred days and celebrations in Islam.

Fajr
Dhuhur
'Asr
Maghrib
'Isha

Zakat
(Giving to Those in Need)

Zakat is the third pillar of Islam and teaches Muslims the importance of sharing their blessings with others. The word Zakat means purification and growth. By giving a portion of their wealth to people in need, Muslims purify their hearts from greed and help their communities grow stronger.

Muslims who are able give part of their savings each year to help the poor, the hungry, and those facing difficulties. This act of charity reminds everyone that wealth is a gift from Allah and should be used with kindness and responsibility. It also helps create fairness and compassion within society.

Zakat is especially important during Ramadan, when many Muslims increase their acts of charity. Before Eid al Fitr, families often give a special charity called Zakat al Fitr, making sure everyone can join in the celebration with food and joy. In this way, charity becomes part of the happiness of special Islamic events.

Through Zakat, Muslims learn generosity, empathy, and gratitude. Children who grow up understanding charity learn to care about others and to help whenever they can. This pillar shows that faith is not only about prayer, but also about kindness in action.

Sawm
(Fasting During Ramadan)

Sawm is the fourth pillar of Islam and means fasting during the holy month of Ramadan. From dawn until sunset, Muslims do not eat or drink. Fasting is a special act of worship that teaches patience, self control, and gratitude for the blessings Allah provides every day.

During Ramadan, Muslims wake up before sunrise for a meal called Suhoor, which gives them strength for the day ahead. When the sun sets, they break their fast with Iftar, often beginning with dates and water, just as Prophet Muhammad taught. Families gather together at this joyful time, sharing meals, prayers, and kindness.

Fasting is not only about staying away from food and drink. It is also about being thoughtful, speaking kindly, helping others, and remembering Allah more often. Muslims spend extra time reading the Quran, praying, and giving charity during this blessed month. These acts make Ramadan one of the most special times of the Islamic year.

Sawm helps Muslims understand patience, discipline, and compassion for those who may not always have enough to eat. It prepares the heart for the celebration of Eid al Fitr, which comes at the end of Ramadan. For children, learning about fasting also teaches the deeper meaning behind one of Islam's most cherished events.

Hajj
(The Pilgrimage to Mecca)

Hajj is the fifth pillar of Islam and one of the most important journeys a Muslim can make. It is the pilgrimage to the holy city of Mecca, which every Muslim who is able should perform at least once in their lifetime. Each year, millions of Muslims from around the world travel there to worship Allah together.

During Hajj, pilgrims wear simple white clothing called Ihram, showing that all people are equal before Allah. Rich and poor, young and old, people from many nations stand side by side in prayer. This reminds Muslims that faith brings everyone together as one community.

Pilgrims perform many sacred rituals during Hajj. They circle the Kaaba in a worship act called Tawaf, walk between the hills of Safa and Marwah, and spend time in deep prayer on the Day of Arafah. These acts remember the faith, patience, and devotion of Prophet Ibrahim and his family.

Hajj teaches humility, unity, sacrifice, and complete devotion to Allah. It is closely connected to Eid al Adha, the joyful celebration that follows the pilgrimage days. For children, learning about Hajj opens the door to understanding one of the most powerful and beautiful events in Islam.

Sacred Months and Times

The Islamic year is filled with special months and sacred times that help Muslims remember Allah and reflect on their faith. Some months mark the beginning of a new year, others are filled with fasting, prayer, charity, and pilgrimage. These blessed times guide Muslims through moments of patience, gratitude, sacrifice, and devotion.

In this section, readers will explore the sacred month of Muharram, the blessed month of Ramadan, and the important days of Dhul Hijjah. Each chapter shows how these months shape the Islamic calendar and prepare Muslims for some of the most meaningful events in Islam.

The Month of Muharram

Muharram is the first month of the Islamic calendar, making it a very special time for Muslims around the world. It marks the beginning of the new Islamic year and reminds Muslims of reflection, gratitude, and new beginnings. Because it is one of the sacred months in Islam, it is honored with respect and devotion.

One of the most important days in Muharram is the Day of Ashura, which falls on the tenth day of the month. Many Muslims fast on this day to remember how Allah saved Prophet Musa and his people from Pharaoh. It is a day of gratitude, prayer, and remembering Allah's mercy.

Muharram is also a time when Muslims think about important moments in Islamic history, including the Hijrah, the migration of Prophet Muhammad, peace be upon him, from Mecca to Medina. This journey led to the beginning of the Islamic calendar and the growth of the Muslim community.

For children, Muharram teaches the beauty of starting a new year with faith and good intentions. It reminds Muslims to be thankful for Allah's guidance and to begin each new year with kindness, prayer, and hope.

1
MUHARRAM

The Month of Ramadan

Ramadan is the ninth month of the Islamic calendar and one of the holiest times in Islam. During this blessed month, Muslims fast from dawn until sunset, spend extra time in prayer, and focus on kindness and gratitude. It is a month filled with worship, family, and spiritual growth.

Each day of Ramadan begins before sunrise with a meal called Suhoor. After fasting throughout the day, families gather at sunset for Iftar, the meal that breaks the fast. Homes and mosques are often filled with joy as people share food, pray together, and thank Allah for His blessings.

Ramadan is also the month in which the Quran was first revealed to Prophet Muhammad, peace be upon him. Because of this, Muslims spend extra time reading the Quran and praying special night prayers called Taraweeh. The last ten nights are especially sacred, as they include Laylat al Qadr, the Night of Power.

For children, Ramadan is a beautiful time to learn patience, generosity, and compassion. Even those who are too young to fast can join in by helping others, praying, and sharing meals with family. The month ends with the joyful celebration of Eid al Fitr, making Ramadan one of the most cherished times of the year.

RAMADAN

The Month of Dhul Hijjah

Dhul Hijjah is the twelfth and final month of the Islamic calendar, and it is one of the most sacred times in Islam. This blessed month is especially important because it is the time when Muslims perform Hajj, the great pilgrimage to Mecca. It is a month filled with worship, sacrifice, and remembrance of Allah.

The first ten days of Dhul Hijjah are considered among the most blessed days of the year. During this time, Muslims increase their prayers, give charity, and do many good deeds. These days lead to the Day of Arafah, when pilgrims stand in prayer and reflection, asking Allah for mercy and forgiveness.

Dhul Hijjah is also the month of Eid al Adha, the Festival of Sacrifice. This joyful celebration honors the devotion of Prophet Ibrahim, who was willing to obey Allah completely. Families gather for prayer, share meals, and give meat to relatives, friends, and those in need.

For children, Dhul Hijjah teaches the values of faith, sacrifice, and generosity. It reminds Muslims that some of the most meaningful moments in Islam come from devotion, sharing, and remembering Allah together as a community.

DHUL HIJJAH

The Blessed Nights

Some of the most special moments in Islam happen during the quiet and sacred hours of the night. These blessed nights are filled with prayer, reflection, wonder, and closeness to Allah. They remind Muslims that even in the stillness of darkness, faith can shine brightly through worship and remembrance.

In this section, readers will discover Laylat al Qadr, the Night of Power, and Isra and Miraj, the miraculous Night Journey of Prophet Muhammad, peace be upon him. These chapters reveal nights of divine mercy, heavenly signs, and some of the most beloved moments in Islamic history.

Laylat al Qadr
(The Night of Power)

Laylat al Qadr is one of the most sacred nights in Islam. Its name means The Night of Power or The Night of Decree, and it takes place during the last ten nights of Ramadan. Muslims believe this is the blessed night when the first verses of the Quran were revealed to Prophet Muhammad, peace be upon him.

On this special night, Muslims spend extra time praying, reading the Quran, and asking Allah for forgiveness and mercy. Many stay awake late into the night in worship, filling their hearts with peace and hope. It is believed that worship on this one night is better than worship over many months and years.

Laylat al Qadr teaches Muslims the value of quiet reflection and sincere prayer. Families often go to the mosque together, and children may join by listening to Quran recitation, making simple prayers, or staying awake a little longer than usual. The night feels peaceful, meaningful, and full of blessings.

For children, Laylat al Qadr is a reminder that some moments in life are especially precious. It teaches that a single night of sincere prayer, kindness, and faith can hold great reward. This makes it one of the most cherished nights in the Islamic year.

Isra and Miraj

Isra and Miraj is one of the most amazing events in Islamic history. On this blessed night, Allah took Prophet Muhammad, peace be upon him, on a miraculous journey from Mecca to Jerusalem, and then through the heavens. This special event showed Allah's power and honored the Prophet with a journey unlike any other.

The first part of the journey is called Isra, when the Prophet traveled by night to the sacred mosque in Jerusalem. The second part is called Miraj, when he ascended through the heavens and met earlier prophets along the way. During this journey, he was shown many signs of Allah's greatness and mercy.

One of the most important gifts from this night was the command for Muslims to pray the five daily prayers. This is why Salat is so deeply connected to Isra and Miraj. The event reminds Muslims that prayer is a precious gift that helps them stay close to Allah every day.

For children, Isra and Miraj is a story of faith, wonder, and trust in Allah. It teaches that Allah can do all things and that special moments in Islamic history often bring blessings for all Muslims. This makes the Night Journey one of the most beloved stories in Islam.

The Great Celebrations

Some of the most joyful moments in Islam are the great celebrations that bring families and communities together. These special days are filled with prayer, gratitude, delicious food, beautiful clothes, and acts of generosity. They remind Muslims that after worship, patience, and sacrifice come moments of happiness and sharing.

In this section, readers will explore Eid al Fitr, the celebration that comes after Ramadan, and Eid al Adha, the Festival of Sacrifice during Dhul Hijjah. These chapters show how Muslims around the world celebrate with prayer, family gatherings, gifts, charity, and kindness.

Eid al Fitr
(The Festival of Breaking the Fast)

Eid al Fitr is the joyful celebration that marks the end of Ramadan. After a whole month of fasting, prayer, and kindness, Muslims around the world come together to thank Allah and celebrate. It is one of the happiest days in the Islamic year, filled with smiles, family, and gratitude.

The day begins with a special Eid prayer, where families gather in mosques or large open spaces. People wear their best clothes, greet one another warmly, and say "Eid Mubarak," which means "Blessed Eid." Before the prayer, many families give a special charity called Zakat al Fitr, making sure everyone can share in the joy of the day.

After prayer, homes are often filled with delicious food, sweets, and happy visitors. Children may receive gifts, new clothes, or money called Eidi. Families visit relatives and friends, share meals, and spend the day celebrating the blessings of Ramadan.

For children, Eid al Fitr is a wonderful reminder that patience and worship are followed by joy and reward. It teaches gratitude, generosity, and the happiness of sharing special moments with loved ones. This makes Eid one of the most cherished celebrations in Islam.

Eid al Adha
(The Festival of Sacrifice)

Eid al Adha is one of the most important celebrations in Islam. It takes place during the blessed month of Dhul Hijjah, around the same time as Hajj. This special day honors the devotion of Prophet Ibrahim, who was willing to obey Allah completely.

The celebration begins with a special Eid prayer, where Muslims gather with family and community. People wear beautiful clothes, greet one another with "Eid Mubarak," and thank Allah for His blessings. The day is filled with prayer, joy, and remembrance.

A very important part of Eid al Adha is the act of sacrifice, usually a sheep, goat, or other animal. The meat is then shared in three parts: one for the family, one for relatives and friends, and one for people in need. This teaches generosity, kindness, and the importance of caring for others.

For children, Eid al Adha is a beautiful lesson in faith, obedience, and sharing. It reminds Muslims of Prophet Ibrahim's trust in Allah and shows that true devotion is connected with generosity and compassion. This makes it one of the most meaningful celebrations in Islam.

Pilgrimage Events

The pilgrimage to Mecca is one of the most meaningful journeys in Islam. It is a path filled with prayer, devotion, movement, and remembrance of Allah. Each step of Hajj teaches lessons of humility, unity, sacrifice, and trust, allowing Muslims to feel deeply connected to their faith.

In this section, readers will follow the sacred journey from preparing for Hajj to entering Ihram, performing Tawaf, standing on the Day of Arafah, and completing the final acts of sacrifice and celebration. These chapters bring the pilgrimage to life as a step by step journey of faith.

Preparing for Hajj

Preparing for Hajj is an exciting and meaningful time for Muslims who are about to make the sacred journey to Mecca. Before leaving, pilgrims learn about the rituals they will perform, gather the things they need, and make their intentions sincere for Allah. This preparation helps them begin the journey with focus, humility, and devotion.

Pilgrims often spend time asking forgiveness, settling any debts, and saying goodbye to family and friends. Because Hajj is such an important event, many people prepare their hearts as much as their travel bags. They pray for a safe journey and ask Allah to accept their worship.

One important part of preparation is learning about Ihram, the simple white clothing worn during Hajj. Men wear two plain white cloths, while women dress modestly and simply. These clothes remind pilgrims that everyone stands equal before Allah, no matter where they come from or what they own.

For children, preparing for Hajj teaches that important journeys begin with the right intention and a humble heart. It shows that worship is not only about the destination, but also about getting ready with sincerity, patience, and faith.

PASSPORT

Entering the State of Ihram

Before pilgrims begin the sacred rituals of Hajj, they enter a special state called Ihram. This is a state of purity, focus, and devotion to Allah. It begins with making the intention for Hajj and preparing both the body and the heart for worship.

Pilgrims wear simple clothing to show humility and equality. Men wear two plain white cloths, while women dress modestly in simple garments. Without fancy clothes or signs of wealth, everyone looks similar, reminding Muslims that all people are equal before Allah.

While in Ihram, pilgrims follow special rules that help them stay focused on worship. They avoid arguments, harmful actions, and anything that distracts from their devotion. Instead, they spend their time praying, remembering Allah, and repeating the beautiful words of the Talbiyah, declaring their readiness to answer Allah's call.

For children, Ihram teaches an important lesson about simplicity and purity of intention. It shows that when Muslims worship Allah, what matters most is the sincerity of the heart, not the things a person owns or wears.

Tawaf

One of the most important rituals of Hajj is Tawaf, which means circling the Kaaba. The Kaaba is the sacred house in Mecca toward which Muslims pray every day. During Tawaf, pilgrims walk around it seven times, moving together in worship and remembrance of Allah.

As they circle the Kaaba, pilgrims make prayers, ask for forgiveness, and thank Allah for His blessings. The sight of thousands of people moving together in harmony is powerful and beautiful. It reminds Muslims that they are all united in faith, no matter where they come from.

Tawaf is not only part of Hajj. Many Muslims also perform it during Umrah, the smaller pilgrimage that can be made at any time of the year. This act of circling the Kaaba connects worshippers to Prophet Ibrahim and the long history of devotion in Islam.

For children, Tawaf teaches unity, devotion, and the beauty of worshiping together. It shows how millions of hearts can be focused on one purpose: remembering Allah with love, humility, and gratitude.

The Day of Arafah

The Day of Arafah is one of the most important days in Islam. During Hajj, pilgrims gather on the plain of Arafah, standing in prayer and asking Allah for mercy and forgiveness. This is often seen as the most meaningful part of the pilgrimage.

From morning until sunset, pilgrims spend their time making dua, remembering Allah, and reflecting on their lives. They pray with sincerity, hoping for forgiveness and blessings. The day is filled with humility, peace, and deep devotion.

Even Muslims who are not on Hajj often observe this day by fasting and praying. Many believe it is a day of great mercy, when prayers are especially meaningful. This makes the Day of Arafah important for Muslims all around the world.

For children, the Day of Arafah teaches the beauty of sincere prayer and asking Allah for guidance. It reminds Muslims that some of the most powerful moments in faith come from standing humbly before Allah with an open heart.

The Stoning of the Pillars

After the Day of Arafah, pilgrims take part in an important ritual called the Stoning of the Pillars. In this act, they throw small pebbles at three stone pillars in Mina. This ritual remembers how Prophet Ibrahim rejected the whispers of Shaytan and stayed firm in obeying Allah.

Each pebble reminds pilgrims to turn away from temptation and choose what is right. The act is not about anger, but about showing strength in faith and resisting anything that pulls a person away from Allah. It is a powerful lesson in courage and self control.

The stoning ritual also teaches that every Muslim faces choices in life. Just as Prophet Ibrahim stayed strong, Muslims are reminded to choose honesty, kindness, and obedience to Allah even when it is difficult. This makes the ritual meaningful far beyond the pilgrimage itself.

For children, the Stoning of the Pillars is a memorable way to understand standing up against wrong choices. It teaches bravery, discipline, and the importance of following what is good and true.

The Sacrifice and Celebration

After the rituals of Hajj, pilgrims take part in the act of sacrifice, remembering the devotion of Prophet Ibrahim. This special moment honors his willingness to obey Allah completely. It reminds Muslims that faith is shown through trust, devotion, and obedience.

The meat from the sacrifice is shared generously with family, friends, and people in need. This teaches Muslims that worship should always be connected to kindness and helping others. Sharing the blessings of food makes the celebration meaningful for the whole community.

This day also brings the joyful celebration of Eid al Adha, when Muslims gather for prayer, wear their best clothes, and spend time with loved ones. Homes are filled with delicious meals, warm greetings, and acts of generosity. It is a time of happiness after the sacred journey.

For children, this chapter teaches that worship often ends with gratitude, sharing, and joy. It shows that important events in Islam are not only about rituals, but also about love, community, and caring for others.

Important Historical Events

Islamic history is filled with powerful moments that shaped the faith and guided Muslims for generations. These events tell stories of courage, revelation, migration, community, and forgiveness. They help readers understand how Islam grew and how its teachings spread across the world.

In this section, readers will discover the First Revelation, the Hijrah to Medina, the building of the first mosque, and the peaceful Conquest of Mecca. These chapters bring history to life through stories of faith, perseverance, and mercy.

The First Revelation

One of the most important events in Islam is the First Revelation, when Allah sent the first verses of the Quran to Prophet Muhammad, peace be upon him. This happened in the Cave of Hira, near Mecca, where the Prophet often went for quiet reflection and prayer.

One night, the angel Jibril appeared and brought Allah's message. He said, "Read!" even though Prophet Muhammad could not read. With Allah's help, the first verses of the Quran were revealed, beginning a message that would guide millions of people around the world.

This event marked the beginning of Islam's holy book, the Quran, and changed history forever. It was the start of Prophet Muhammad's mission to teach people about worshiping Allah alone, being kind, honest, and just, and following the path of righteousness.

For children, the First Revelation teaches the beauty of knowledge, guidance, and trust in Allah's wisdom. It reminds Muslims that the Quran began with a moment of wonder and divine mercy, making it one of the most sacred events in Islamic history.

The Migration to Medina
(Hijrah)

One of the most important rituals of Hajj is Tawaf, which means circling the Kaaba. The Kaaba is the sacred house in Mecca toward which Muslims pray every day. During Tawaf, pilgrims walk around it seven times, moving together in worship and remembrance of Allah.

As they circle the Kaaba, pilgrims make prayers, ask for forgiveness, and thank Allah for His blessings. The sight of thousands of people moving together in harmony is powerful and beautiful. It reminds Muslims that they are all united in faith, no matter where they come from.

Tawaf is not only part of Hajj. Many Muslims also perform it during Umrah, the smaller pilgrimage that can be made at any time of the year. This act of circling the Kaaba connects worshippers to Prophet Ibrahim and the long history of devotion in Islam.

For children, Tawaf teaches unity, devotion, and the beauty of worshiping together. It shows how millions of hearts can be focused on one purpose: remembering Allah with love, humility, and gratitude.

The Building of the First Mosque

After arriving in Medina, one of the first things Prophet Muhammad, peace be upon him, did was help build a mosque. This became the first mosque of the Muslim community, a special place for prayer, learning, and gathering together. It showed that worship and community were at the heart of Muslim life.

The Prophet worked alongside his companions, helping carry stones and build with his own hands. This taught Muslims the importance of humility, teamwork, and serving the community. The mosque was not only a place to pray, but also a place where people learned about Islam and supported one another.

From this first mosque, the Muslim community grew stronger. People came together for the daily prayers, for Jumuah on Fridays, and to learn the teachings of the Quran. It became the center of faith, friendship, and guidance in Medina.

For children, the building of the first mosque teaches that strong communities are built through cooperation, kindness, and shared faith. It reminds Muslims that a mosque is much more than a building. It is a place where hearts come together in worship and peace.

The Conquest of Mecca

The Conquest of Mecca was one of the most important events in Islamic history. After many years, Prophet Muhammad, peace be upon him, returned to Mecca with his followers. This was the city where Islam first began and where the Prophet had once faced great hardship.

When the Muslims entered Mecca, many people expected anger or revenge. Instead, Prophet Muhammad showed mercy and forgiveness. He forgave the people who had once opposed him and called them toward peace and worship of Allah. This act of kindness became one of the most powerful lessons in Islamic history.

During this event, the idols around the Kaaba were removed, and the sacred house was once again dedicated to the worship of Allah alone. Mecca became the spiritual center of Islam, and Muslims everywhere turned toward it in prayer.

For children, the Conquest of Mecca teaches that true strength comes from forgiveness and compassion. It reminds Muslims that even after difficult times, peace and mercy can bring hearts together and create new beginnings.

Special Weekly and Daily Practices

Faith in Islam is not only remembered during great annual events, but also through weekly and daily acts of worship and kindness. These regular practices help Muslims stay connected to Allah throughout the year and make faith a natural part of everyday life.

In this section, readers will explore the special Friday prayer of Jumuah, the beauty of Sadaqah, and the importance of acts of kindness. These chapters show how even small actions can carry great meaning in Islam.

Jumuah
The Friday Prayer

Jumuah is the special Friday prayer that Muslims gather for every week. It takes place around midday and replaces the regular Dhuhr prayer on Fridays. For Muslims, Friday is a blessed day filled with worship, community, and reflection.

Before Jumuah, Muslims often prepare by washing, wearing clean clothes, and going early to the mosque. Families and friends gather together, and the mosque becomes full of people ready to pray. This weekly gathering reminds Muslims of the importance of unity and shared faith.

During Jumuah, the imam gives a khutbah, or sermon, teaching lessons from the Quran and reminding everyone about kindness, honesty, and devotion to Allah. After listening carefully, the congregation prays together in rows, standing shoulder to shoulder in worship.

For children, Jumuah teaches the joy of gathering with the community each week. It reminds Muslims that faith is strengthened not only during great annual events, but also through regular worship, learning, and friendship.

FRIDAY
JUMUAH

Giving Charity

Sadaqah is the voluntary charity that Muslims give out of kindness and love for others. Unlike Zakat, which is one of the Five Pillars, Sadaqah can be given at any time and in many different ways. It teaches that helping others is a beautiful part of everyday faith.

Sadaqah does not always have to be money. Sharing food, helping someone in need, smiling kindly, or offering support are also forms of charity in Islam. This helps children understand that even small acts of kindness can have great meaning.

Many Muslims increase their Sadaqah during Ramadan, Eid, and the first days of Dhul Hijjah, but it can be practiced all year long. These acts of giving strengthen communities and remind everyone to care for one another.

For children, Sadaqah teaches generosity, empathy, and love. It shows that every good deed, no matter how small, can bring happiness to others and reward from Allah. This makes charity one of the most beautiful daily practices in Islam.

Acts of Kindness in Islam

Kindness is one of the most beautiful teachings in Islam. Muslims are encouraged to be gentle, helpful, and caring in their words and actions every day. Whether it is helping a family member, sharing with a friend, or showing respect to a neighbor, every act of kindness is valued by Allah.

The teachings of Prophet Muhammad, peace be upon him, are filled with examples of kindness. He taught Muslims to smile, speak gently, care for the poor, and even show mercy to animals. These lessons remind children that faith is shown not only in prayer, but also in how people treat others.

Acts of kindness are especially meaningful during important events like Ramadan, Eid, and Hajj, when Muslims often help more people and strengthen their communities. Yet Islam also teaches that kindness should continue every day of the year, making life better for everyone.

For children, this chapter teaches that even the smallest good deed can have great meaning. A kind word, a helping hand, or a caring heart can brighten someone's day and bring reward from Allah. This makes kindness one of the most powerful ways to live the teachings of Islam.

Final
Reflections

The journey through the important events in Islam does not truly end with the last page of the book. The lessons of prayer, kindness, sacrifice, charity, and gratitude continue every day in the lives of Muslims around the world.

In this final section, readers will reflect on Living a Life of Faith and Remembering Allah Every Day, bringing together all the beautiful lessons learned throughout the book.

Living a Life of Faith

The important events in Islam teach Muslims how to live with faith, kindness, gratitude, and devotion to Allah. From the sacred month of Ramadan to the joyful celebrations of Eid, from the journey of Hajj to the weekly gathering of Jumuah, each event helps Muslims remember what truly matters in life.

These special days and practices are more than moments on a calendar. They are opportunities to grow closer to Allah, strengthen family bonds, help those in need, and build caring communities. Each event carries lessons of patience, generosity, sacrifice, forgiveness, and love.

For children, learning about these events helps them understand that Islam is a way of life filled with beautiful traditions and meaningful moments. Every prayer, every act of charity, and every celebration becomes part of a lifelong journey of faith.

As this book comes to an end, may its lessons inspire readers to carry kindness, gratitude, and remembrance of Allah into every day of their lives. In this way, the important events of Islam continue to shine in the heart long after the special days have passed.

Remembering Allah Every Day

Remembering Allah every day is one of the most beautiful parts of a Muslim's life. While special events like Ramadan, Eid, and Hajj come at certain times of the year, a Muslim's connection to Allah continues every single day. Through prayer, gratitude, good deeds, and kind words, Muslims keep their hearts close to their Creator.

There are many simple ways Muslims remember Allah in daily life. They say Bismillah before beginning something, Alhamdulillah when they are thankful, and SubhanAllah when they think about Allah's greatness. These small words of remembrance fill everyday moments with faith and meaning.

Remembering Allah also means living in a way that pleases Him. Helping others, speaking gently, being honest, showing patience, and caring for family are all ways of keeping faith alive each day. In this way, worship is not limited to special times, but becomes part of daily life.

For children, remembering Allah every day teaches that faith is not only about big events, but also about small, beautiful moments. A thankful heart, a kind action, and a simple prayer can all bring a person closer to Allah. This is how the lessons of Islam stay bright in the heart all year long.

You May Also Like

Continue your journey through the beauty of Islam with another inspiring book for young readers.

The 25 Prophets
An Introduction to the Prophets of Islam

Discover The 25 Prophets, from Adam to Muhammad, and learn the lessons of faith, patience, courage, and trust in Allah that continue to inspire Muslims around the world.

Perfect for children and families who enjoyed **Sacred Events in Islam.**

Copyright

Published by Shoebill LLC

ISBN: 979-8-90359-004-9

For permissions, business inquiries, or bulk orders, please contact:
info@shoebill.com

www.shoebill.com